W9-AAW-182

# Let's Experiment with Science

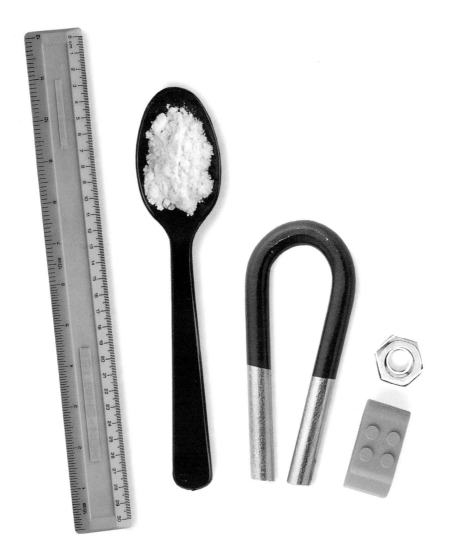

# Let's Experiment
# with Science

JACK CHALLONER and ANGELA WILKES

# How to use this book

**Let's Experiment with Science** is full of interesting projects to try at home, from testing magnets to making an incredible bottle volcano. Below are the points to look out for when using this book and a list of things to remember.

### Equipment
Illustrated checklists show you which tools to have ready before you start a project.

### The things you need
The materials to collect for each project are clearly shown to help you check that you have everything you need.

### Step-by-step
Step-by-step photographs and clear instructions tell you exactly what to do at each stage of a project.

## Things to remember

- Read through all the instructions and gather together everything you will need before you begin a project.

- Put on an apron, roll up your sleeves, and cover your work area with newspaper before you start.

- Follow the instructions carefully at each stage of the experiment and only do one thing at a time.

- Be very careful with sharp scissors. Do not use them unless there is an adult there to help you.

- Keep a record of each experiment or project and note down the results of your tests.

- When you have finished, put everything away, clean up any mess, and wash your hands.

A DK PUBLISHING BOOK

**U.S. Editor** Camela Decaire
**Editor** Fiona Campbell
**Assistant Designer** Caroline Potts
**Managing Editor** Jane Yorke
**Managing Art Editor** Chris Scollen
**Production** David Hyde
**Photography** Dave King and Mike Dunning
**Illustrator** Brian Delf

First American Edition, 1996
2 4 6 8 10 9 7 5 3

Published in the United States by
DK Publishing, Inc., 95 Madison Avenue,
New York, New York 10016
Visit us on the World Wide Web at http://www.dk.com

A CIP catalog record for this book is available from the Library of Congress.

ISBN 0-7894-1273-X

Color reproduction by Colourscan
Printed and bound in Italy by L.E.G.O.

# CONTENTS

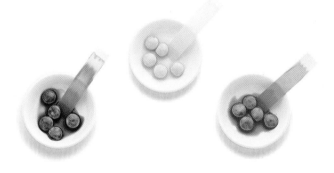

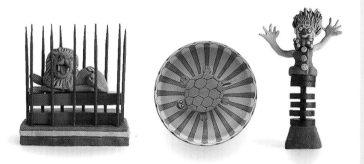

# WATER FILTER

We expect clean drinking water whenever we turn on the faucet. But because most of our drinking water comes from rivers, reservoirs, and under the ground, it often starts off dirty. It has run through rocks and soil, and can contain the wastes of animals and plants, and polluting chemicals. To make it safe to drink, the water that we use in our homes has to be specially cleaned at a water purification plant. Try constructing this water filter to find out how it is done.

*A pitcher of water*

*Soil*

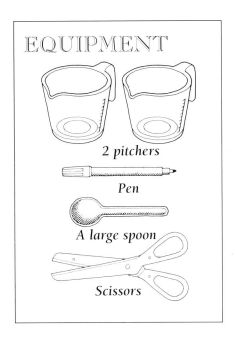

## EQUIPMENT

2 pitchers

Pen

A large spoon

Scissors

## You will need

*Grass and leaves*

*Gravel or small pebbles*

*Coarse sand*

*Blotting paper*

*A clean flowerpot*

# Making the water filter

1 Spoon some small amounts of soil, sand, gravel, grass, and leaves into the pitcher of water. Stir everything together.

2 Stand the flowerpot on the blotting paper and draw around the base of the pot. Cut the circle out of the blotting paper.

3 Put the circle of blotting paper at the bottom of the flowerpot. Fill the pot halfway with sand, then add a layer of gravel.

# Using the water filter

Stand the flowerpot filter on top of an empty pitcher. Slowly pour the muddy water into the filter.

# What happens

*The water that runs out of the filter is cleaner than the water poured in because the filter traps a lot of dirt. The filters at a purification plant are very thick and make water much cleaner. Then special chemicals are added to the water to kill any germs.*

Muddy water

*Flowerpot filter*

*The water runs out through the hole in the bottom of the flowerpot filter.*

*Cleaner, filtered water*

*DO NOT DRINK THE FILTERED WATER!*

# BOTTLE VOLCANO

Have you ever noticed that the first few sips of a hot drink always seem much hotter than the rest of the drink at the bottom of the cup? This simple experiment with water shows in a dramatic way exactly what happens when you mix hot liquids and cold liquids together.

## You will need

*String*

*A small bottle*

*Red food coloring or ink*

*A large glass jar*

EQUIPMENT

*Scissors*

*Paintbrush*

## Setting up the volcano

1 Cut a piece of string about 12 in (30 cm) long. Tie one end of it firmly around the neck of the bottle, leaving the other end free.

2 Tie the other end of the string to the piece tied around the neck of the bottle to make a loop of string for a handle.

3 Fill the large jar with cold water. Don't fill it all the way to the top because you will need space to lower the bottle into it.

4 Fill the small bottle up to the top with hot water. Stir in enough drops of food coloring to turn the water bright red.

5 Hold the small bottle by the string handle and lower it gently into the jar of cold water, being careful to keep it level.

## VOLCANO IN A JAR

As you lower the small bottle into the jar of cold water, the hot water shoots up into the cold water like a volcano. Soon all the hot water will rise to the top of the jar.

## Why hot air rises

*When water is heated, it expands (takes up more space). This makes hot water lighter than cold water, so it rises to the surface.*

# ON THE LEVEL

No two liquids are the same. Have you ever wondered why cream floats on top of milk, or why salad dressing separates into different layers? And did you know that some objects will sink in water, but float on another liquid? In this experiment you can find out some fascinating things about different liquids and create a colorful giant "cocktail" all at the same time.

## You will need

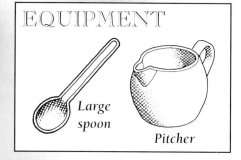

Vegetable oil

Honey

EQUIPMENT

Large spoon

Pitcher

Nuts

Plastic toys

Small metal objects

Water colored with ink or food coloring

Cherry tomatoes

A large, clear plastic container

Dried pasta

Grapes

10

# What to do

1 Carefully pour honey into the container over the back of the spoon until the container is a quarter full.

2 Slowly pour the same amount of vegetable oil into the container. Then add the same amount of colored water.

3 Wait until the liquids have settled into layers. Then gently drop different objects into the container to see what floats.

## LIQUID COCKTAIL

*The liquids separate into three layers, with the honey on the bottom, the water above that, and the oil on top of the water. Liquids do this because some of them are lighter, or less dense, than others. A lighter liquid will float on top of a heavier, or more dense, liquid.*

## Floaters and sinkers

*Some of the objects you drop into the container will sink. Others will float at different levels depending on how heavy they are. Objects float best in dense liquids because these support their weight.*

# SPLITTING COLORS

Many of the inks and dyes that are used to color things are really mixtures of several different-colored chemicals, or *pigments*. The two experiments here show you how to separate the different-colored pigments in felt-tip pens and the food coloring used in candy.

## You will need

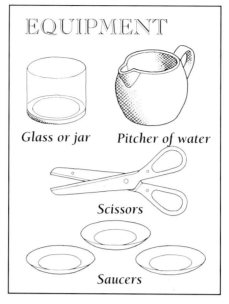

### EQUIPMENT

*Glass or jar*     *Pitcher of water*

*Scissors*

*Saucers*

*Colored felt-tip pens*

*White blotting paper*

*Half a teaspoon of salt*

*Candy-covered chocolates*

## Felt-tip pen test

1 Cut out a rectangle of blotting paper big enough to roll into a tube that you can slide into the glass you are going to use.

2 Make blobs of different colors* about 1½ in (4 cm) from the bottom of the blotting paper with the felt-tip pens.

3 Pour a little water into the glass and stir in the salt. Roll the blotting paper into a tube and stand it in the glass.

12

*\* Dark colors are the most interesting colors to test.*

# Candy test

1 Choose three colors to test. Put five or six candies of the same color in each saucer. Add a few drops of water to each saucer.

2 Turn the candies over and stir them around a little so that most of the color runs off them and colors the water.

3 Cut three strips of blotting paper. Lay a strip in each of the saucers as shown, with one end in the colored water.

## FELT-TIP PEN TEST

*As the water rises up the blotting paper, it dissolves the pigments in the ink blots and carries them up with it. The different pigments move up the paper at different speeds, so they separate, and you can see bands of different colors.*

## CANDY TEST

*The pigments used on the candy are absorbed by the blotting paper in the same way as the pigments in the felt-tip pens. As they move up the blotting paper, they separate. Some of the colors contain only one pigment.*

13

# MAGIC MAGNETS

Magnets have special powers that seem to be magic. Their power is called magnetism, and it can move certain objects around without even touching them. Below you can find out more about magnets, then use their magnetism to do some exciting tricks.

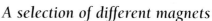

*A selection of different magnets*

**You will need**

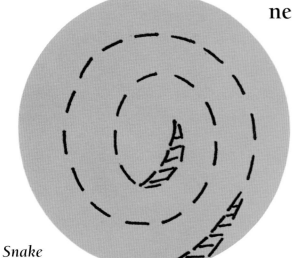

*Snake pattern*

*A variety of small household objects and steel paper clips*

*A ruler*

*Thread*

## Magnetic attraction

Pieces of colored felt

*Glue*

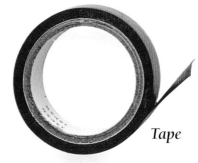

*Tape*

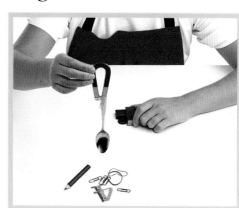

EQUIPMENT

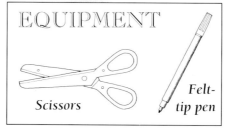

Scissors

Felt-tip pen

Hold a magnet close to each of the objects you have collected. Which objects does the magnet pick up? What are they made of?

# Making the snake

1. Trace the snake pattern on the opposite page, then cut it out in felt. Decorate your snake with small pieces of colored felt.

2. Give the snake felt eyes and a tongue. Tie a short piece of thread to a paper clip. Slide the paper clip onto the snake's head.

3. Tape a magnet to one end of the ruler. Tape the thread from the snake firmly to the table, as shown.

## It's magnetic magic!

### SNAKE CHARMING

Hold the ruler above the snake's head. The magnet pulls the paper clip toward it, and the thread is pulled tight. If you move the magnet around, the snake will dance.

### TOO HEAVY TO HOVER

If the snake is too heavy for your magnet, shorten its thread. If this doesn't work, use a stronger magnet or make a smaller snake.

KITE

The kite is made from a diamond of red felt and colored felt bows. What happens to the kite if you cut its thread?

SNAKE

FLOWER

Yellow felt petals with a blue felt center

Green felt leaves

Tape

### PICK-UP

A magnet will attract (pull toward itself) anything made of iron or steel.

### HOW DOES IT WORK?

The paper clips are attracted to the magnets by magnetism. But because their threads are too short to reach the magnets, the paper clips hover in midair.

# MAGNETIC FIELDS

A magnet's invisible powers are contained within its "magnetic field." You can see the pattern of a magnetic field by putting iron filings near a magnet. Iron filings usually leap toward a magnet, but if you put them in a sticky liquid, such as honey, they will form magnetic patterns very slowly. Stir up the filings every time you use the mixture.

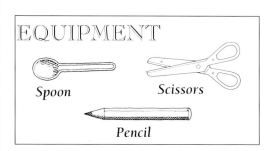

## EQUIPMENT

*Spoon*

*Scissors*

*Pencil*

## You will need

*A selection of different magnets*

*Some string*

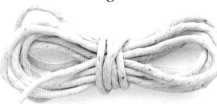

*Iron filings*

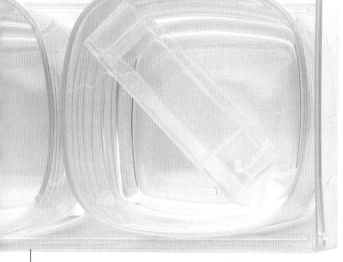

*Clear plastic tubs or glass containers*

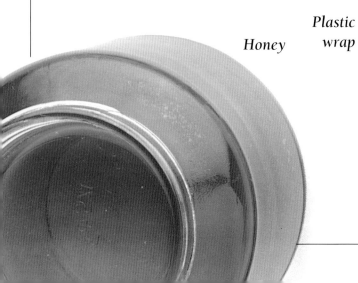

*Honey*

*Plastic wrap*

## Making the mixture

Sprinkle a teaspoonful of iron filings into the honey. Stir gently until the iron filings are evenly mixed into the honey.

## Magnetic patterns

Pour some of the mixture into each tub. Place magnets underneath or at the sides of the tubs, then watch as the magnetic fields appear.

## 3-D fields

Fill a glass with the mixture. Wrap a bar magnet in plastic wrap and tie it to a pencil with string. Hang the magnet in the middle of the glass.

# Fields of filings

*Each magnet forms a magnetic field pattern. Test magnets of different shapes, sizes, and strengths, and compare the fields they make. Then look at the fields you can create when you put two or more magnets near each other. Here are some of the patterns we found.*

## MAGNETIC PATTERNS

*When a magnet is placed near the mixture, the iron filings become magnetized. The filings line up in the field of the magnet, and slide very slowly toward the ends of the magnets, where the magnetism is strongest. When two magnets are near each other, their field patterns change shape.*

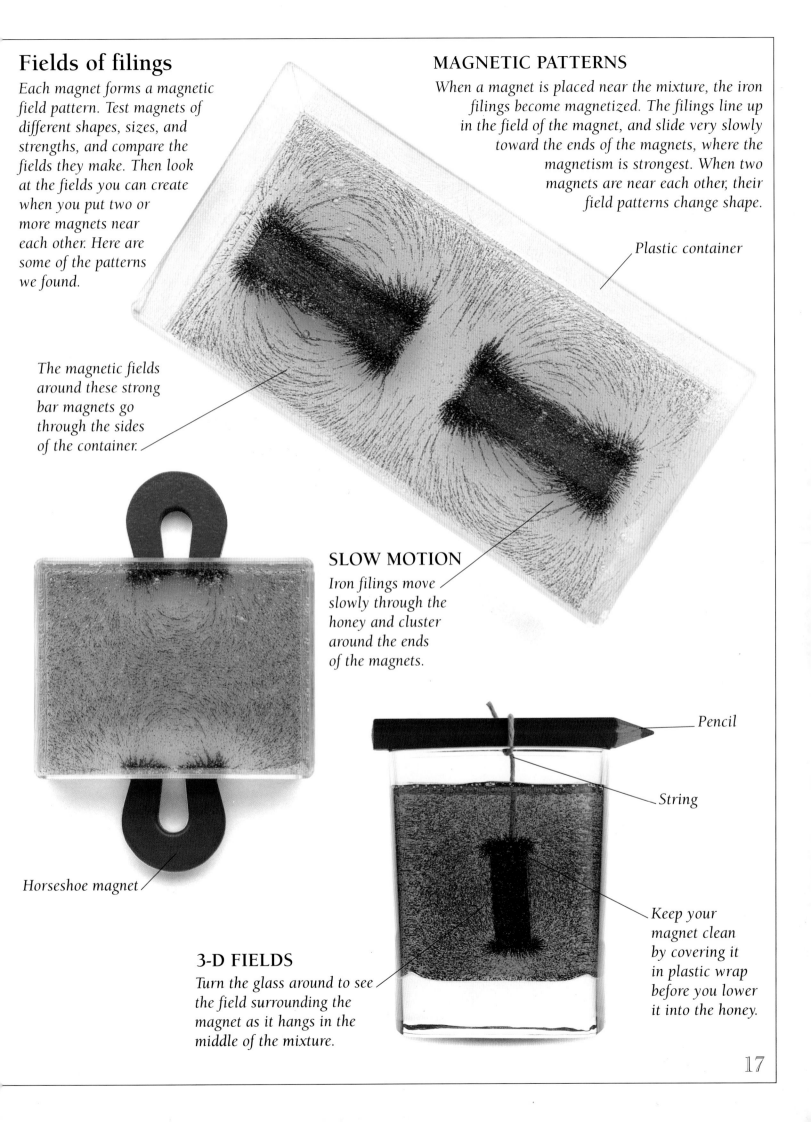

*Plastic container*

*The magnetic fields around these strong bar magnets go through the sides of the container.*

## SLOW MOTION

*Iron filings move slowly through the honey and cluster around the ends of the magnets.*

*Horseshoe magnet*

*Pencil*

*String*

*Keep your magnet clean by covering it in plastic wrap before you lower it into the honey.*

## 3-D FIELDS

*Turn the glass around to see the field surrounding the magnet as it hangs in the middle of the mixture.*

17

# POLES APART

Every magnet has a north pole and a south pole, like the Earth. These poles are the two opposite ends, or sides, of a magnet, where its powers are strongest. You can find out more about magnetic poles, how to identify them and why magnets behave oddly when they are together, in the experiments below. Opposite you can see how to make your own magnets, as well as an amazing turtle compass that really works.

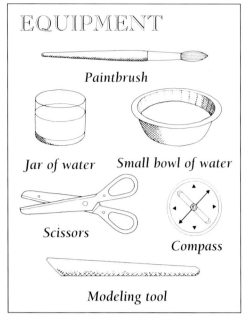

*Poster paint*

*A bottle top*

## EQUIPMENT

*Paintbrush*

*Jar of water*    *Small bowl of water*

*Scissors*

*Compass*

*Modeling tool*

*Wooden skewers*

*A steel needle*

## North or south pole?

*A horseshoe magnet*

## You will need

*Colored modeling clay*

*Strong bar magnets*    *Ring magnets*

Hang a bar magnet about 6 in (7 cm) above the compass.* When it stops moving, the end pointing north is the magnet's north pole.

## Pole position

Try pushing the north poles, then the south poles, of two magnets together. What happens? Next, try a north and a south pole together.

## Making the lion

Paint some skewers, cut them in half, and stick them in some clay around a bar magnet. Model a clay lion. Sit it on another bar magnet.

## Making the clown

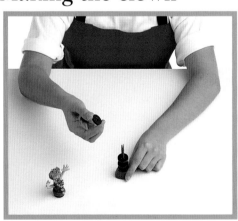

Stick three skewers into some clay. Put some ring magnets onto the skewers. Model a clown from clay and stick it on the top magnet.

*\* The magnet will affect the compass needle if it is too close.*

# Turtle compass

1 Stroke a needle 30 times, from its point to its eye, with the south pole of a magnet. Make a light, flat turtle from clay.

2 Push the turtle onto the open end of the bottle top. Stick the needle point firmly into the turtle's tail, directly opposite its head.

## TURTLE COMPASS

*The needle becomes a magnet when it is stroked by a magnet. As it floats in the bowl, it is affected by the Earth's magnetic field. The turtle's head points to the north and the eye of the needle in its tail points south.*

## BOUNCING CLOWN

*The clown bounces on the invisible magnetic fields of the magnets.*

*The clown's body is hollow so that it is light enough to bounce on the magnets.*

Modeling clay clown

## OPPOSITES ATTRACT...

*The north pole of one magnet and the south pole of another magnet attract (pull toward) each other, and the magnets snap together.*

## ...LIKE POLES REPEL

*Two north poles or two south poles together repel (push away from) each other, so the magnets "float" one above the other.*

Modeling clay base

*Skewer cage bars*

*The top magnet will not float if the lion is too heavy.*

Modeling clay lion

South pole

South pole

North pole

North pole

## LEVITATING LION

*Put the magnet with the lion in the cage, with like poles sitting on top of each other. The magnets* *repel each other, making the top magnet float. Try turning the top magnet, or removing the cage bars.*

19

# KITCHEN CHEMISTRY

You don't need special powders and test tubes to be a chemist. Everything around you is made of chemicals, and you can do all kinds of interesting tests on things around the kitchen. Here and on the next three pages you can find out how to test things to see if they are acid or alkaline.

*Blotting paper*

*Half a lemon*

## You will need

*Baking soda*

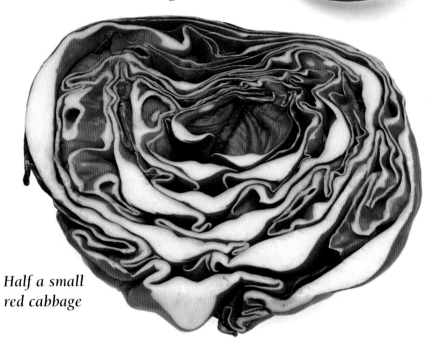

*Water*

*Half a small red cabbage*

## The acid test

1 Chop up the cabbage and put it in a bowl.* Pour hot water over it and leave it to soak until the water turns purple.

2 Hold the sieve over the pitcher. Pour the cabbage water into the pitcher through the sieve.

3 Pour a little purple cabbage water into several of the small jars. Label one jar *Control* and put it to one side.

20      *Ask an adult to help you with the knife.*

# Other things to test

Egg white

Cola drink

## EQUIPMENT

Sieve

Bowl

Cutting board

Teaspoon

Pen or pencil

Knife

Pitcher

Small glasses or jars

Labels

Notebook

Milk of magnesia

Vinegar

A hard candy

A tomato

A slice of apple

Orange juice

Yogurt

Baking powder

Washing soda*

4 Pour a few drops of lemon juice into one of the other jars of purple cabbage water. Label the jar *Lemon juice*.

5 Mix a teaspoon of baking soda with a little water. Stir it into a jar of purple water. Label it *Baking soda*.

6 Do the same with all the other things you want to test. Label every jar to say what is in it as you do each test.

*\* Wash your hands after touching washing soda.*

21

# MAGIC POTIONS

## Changing color

1 Squeeze a little lemon juice into two jars. Mix two teaspoons of baking soda with water in a third jar.

2 Add some purple cabbage water to the two jars of lemon juice. The lemon juice should turn pink. Label one jar *Control*.

3 Add the baking soda water to the pink lemon juice, drop by drop. What happens to the color of the lemon juice?

### THE ACID TEST

### Alkalis
*If the cabbage water turns blue or green, as it does with baking soda, the thing you have tested is an alkali.*

*Lemon*

*Baking soda*

### Control jar
*You keep the Control jar to compare with the tests you do.*

*Purple water with lemon juice added to it*

*Purple water with a candy added to it*

### Acids
*If the purple cabbage water turns pink, as with the lemon juice, the thing you have tested is acid.*

*Purple water with baking soda added to it*

# Other things to test

1 Cut a piece of blotting paper into small strips about ½ in (1.5 cm) wide. Cut a lot of strips so that you can test several liquids.

2 Dip the strips of blotting paper into purple cabbage water, then lay them on a saucer to dry. This may take a few hours.

3 Dip a strip of paper into each liquid you want to test. Try lemon juice, then baking soda mixed with water.

## CHANGING COLOR

*As you add the baking soda (an alkali) to the lemon juice (an acid), the pink water turns purple. This shows that the liquid is no longer acid.*

*Lemon juice*

*Baking soda*

*Strips of indicator paper*

*Purple water with lemon juice added to it*

*Pink water with baking soda added to it*

## MAKING INDICATOR PAPER

*Scientists use "litmus" paper to test liquids to see if they are acid or alkaline. You can make your own. When you dip the indicator paper into an acid, it turns pink. When you dip it into an alkali, it turns blue or green.*

23

# DIRTY WATER TEST

Have you ever wondered where all your water comes from? The fresh water that pours out of our faucets comes from rivers, lakes, streams, reservoirs, and from deep beneath the ground. All living things need water, clean water – but the Earth is like a sponge and soaks up anything liquid that is dumped on the ground or into the rivers. This simple experiment shows you what happens when pollutants get into the water system.

*A stick of celery*

## EQUIPMENT

*3 glass jars*

*Knife*

## You will need

*White flowers*

*Colored ink or food coloring*

*A pitcher of water*

# What to do

1 Pour about 1 in (2 cm) of food coloring or ink into each glass. Add the same amount of water to each glass.

2 Trim the flower and celery stems.* Stand the celery and flowers in colored water and leave them for a few hours.

## HOW YOU CAN HELP

• Encourage your family to use ecologically safe detergent and dishwashing liquid.
• Avoid using chemical fertilizers and pesticides in the garden.
• Tell your parents never to pour chemicals or car oil onto the ground or down a drain.

## DIRTY WATER

*The plants absorb the colored water. The coloring acts like pollution.*

*As the plants drink the water, they drink up any pollution that is in it. This happens to any person or animal that drinks polluted water.*

## WATER POLLUTION

*Factory wastes, pesticides, and fertilizers cause water pollution. But a lot of pollution also starts at home.*

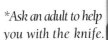

*Ask an adult to help you with the knife.*

# FLYING PAPER

How do airplanes fly? Launch a piece of paper into the air and it will just flutter down to the ground. But if you make a plane with the piece of paper, it will fly really well. Here and on the next three pages you can find out how to make an amazing superglider and a helicopter. They are not only fun to make and play with, but will also teach you a lot about how things fly.

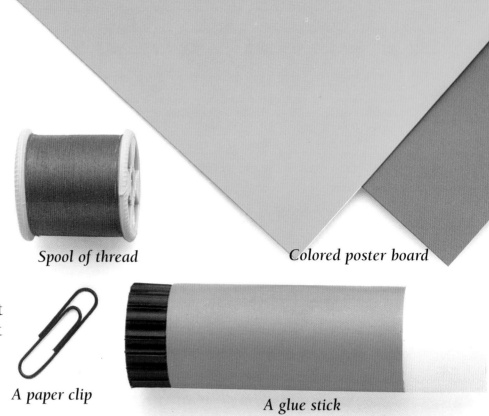

**Spool of thread**

**Colored poster board**

**A paper clip**

**A glue stick**

## You will need

**A drinking straw 7½ in (13 cm) long**

*Tracing paper*

*A small lump of modeling clay*

**String**

EQUIPMENT

*Scissors*

*Ruler*        Pencil

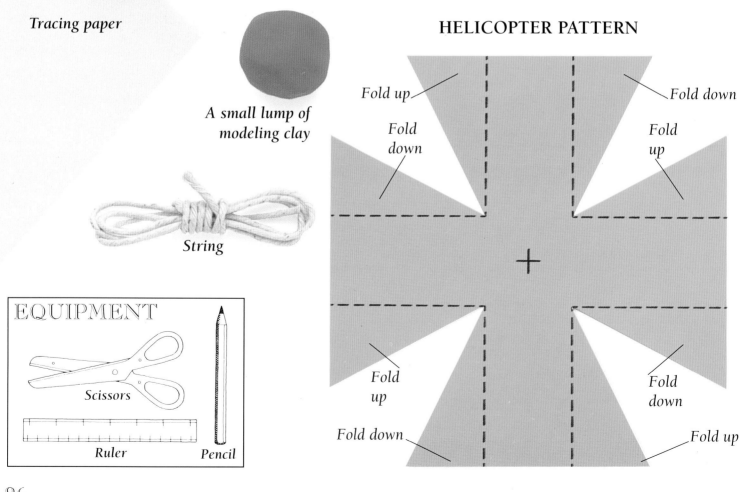

### HELICOPTER PATTERN

*Fold up*

*Fold down*

*Fold down*

*Fold up*

+

*Fold up*

*Fold down*

*Fold down*

*Fold up*

## SUPERGLIDER PATTERN

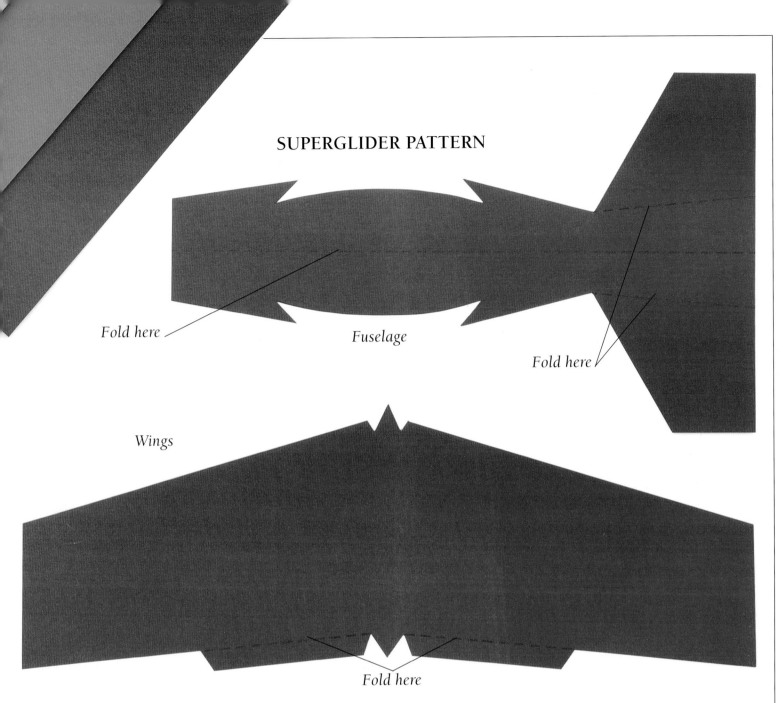

*Fold here*

*Fuselage*

*Fold here*

*Wings*

*Fold here*

# Making the superglider

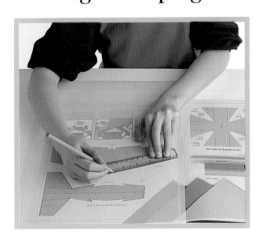

1 Trace the outlines of the two superglider pattern pieces onto tracing paper. Trace along the fold lines using dotted lines.

2 Turn the tracing paper over. Lay it on the poster board and scribble over the lines you have traced to transfer the pattern.

3 Cut the wings and fuselage out of the poster board. Score along the fold lines using your ruler and the point of your scissors.*

*\*This helps make the folds sharper.*

# FLYING HIGH
## Superglider (continued)

4 Fold the fuselage in half along the fold line, then open it out again. Fold down the two tail fins and the two wing flaps.

5 Slot the back of the wings into the back notches on the fuselage. Slot the front of the wings into the front two notches.

6 Put the paper clip on the nose of the airplane. Fold a piece of modeling clay around the paper clip to act as a weight.

## Making the helicopter

1 Trace the pattern for the helicopter rotor onto tracing paper. Trace the fold lines using dotted lines.

2 Turn the tracing paper over. Lay it on the poster board and scribble over the lines you have traced to transfer the pattern.

3 Cut the helicopter rotor out of the poster board. Score along the fold lines using your ruler and the point of your scissors.

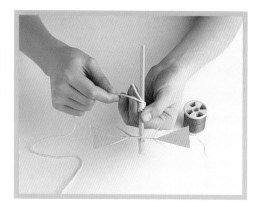

4 Each rotor blade has two fold lines. Fold one side of each rotor blade up and the other side down, along the fold lines.

5 Make a hole in the middle of the rotor.* Spread glue around one end of the straw. Push the straw through the hole in the rotor.

6 Make a loop in one end of the thread. Wind string counter-clockwise over the loop around the straw beneath the rotor.

*Ask an adult to help you.

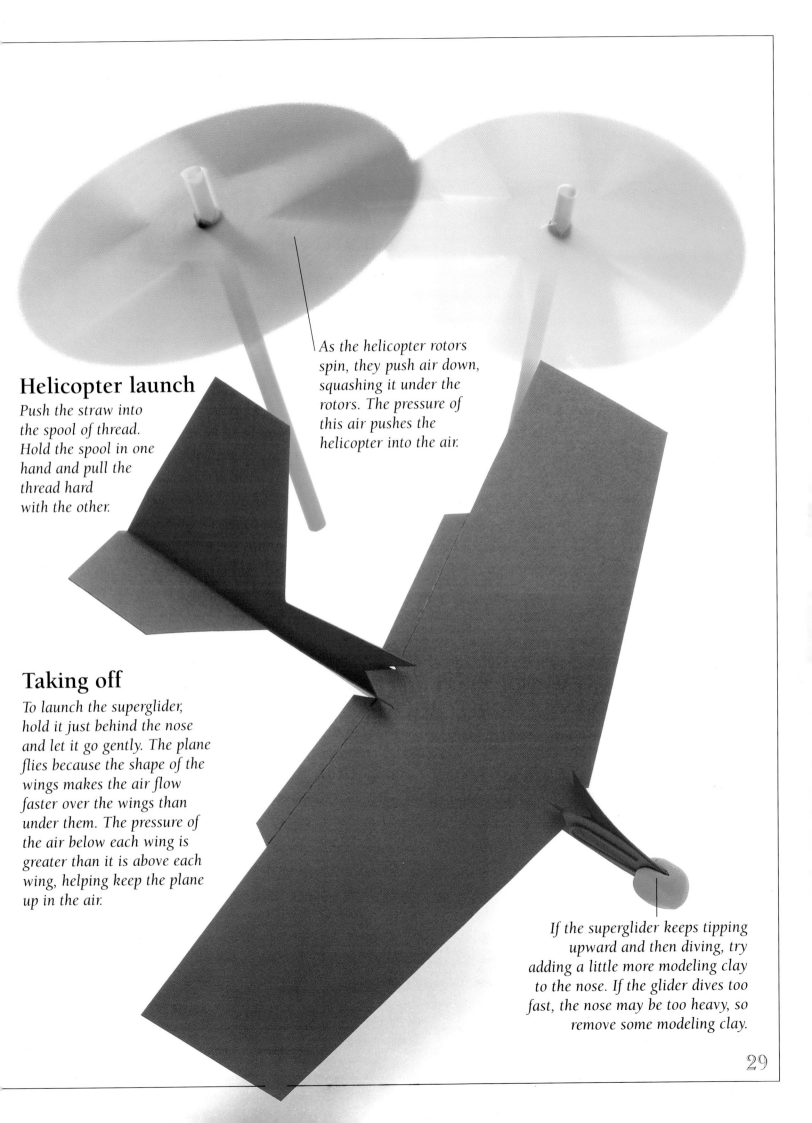

## Helicopter launch

*Push the straw into the spool of thread. Hold the spool in one hand and pull the thread hard with the other.*

*As the helicopter rotors spin, they push air down, squashing it under the rotors. The pressure of this air pushes the helicopter into the air.*

## Taking off

*To launch the superglider, hold it just behind the nose and let it go gently. The plane flies because the shape of the wings makes the air flow faster over the wings than under them. The pressure of the air below each wing is greater than it is above each wing, helping keep the plane up in the air.*

*If the superglider keeps tipping upward and then diving, try adding a little more modeling clay to the nose. If the glider dives too fast, the nose may be too heavy, so remove some modeling clay.*

# VANISHING COLORS

Light looks white, but it is really made of rainbow colors. With this simple multicolored wheel you will be able to make colors disappear, then appear again, as if by magic. Where do the colors go, and why? Spin the wheel, then read about what happens at the bottom of the opposite page.

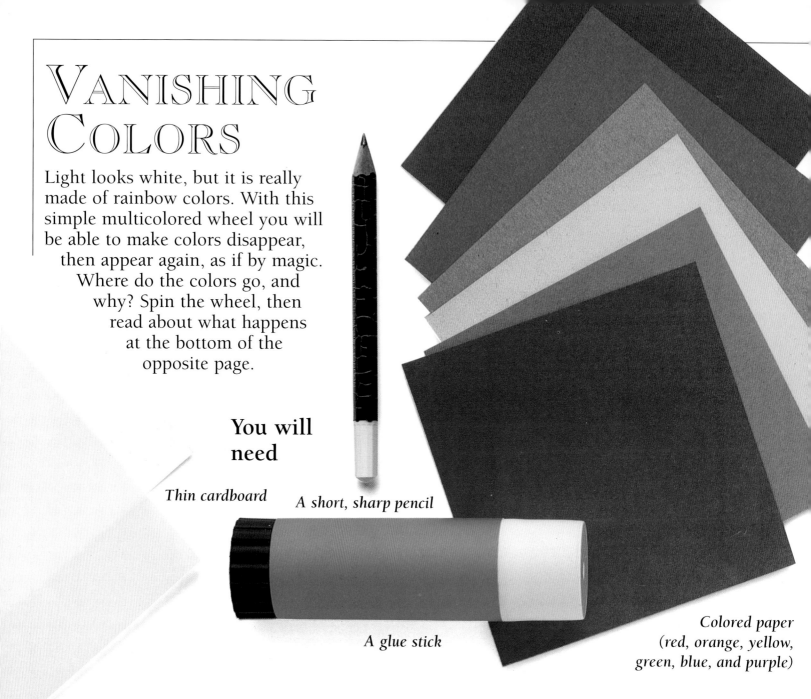

## You will need

*Thin cardboard*

*A short, sharp pencil*

*A glue stick*

*Colored paper (red, orange, yellow, green, blue, and purple)*

*Tracing paper*

## EQUIPMENT

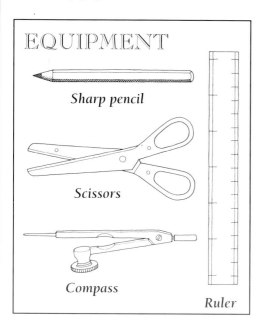

*Sharp pencil*

*Scissors*

*Compass*

*Ruler*

## Making the color wheel

1 Open the compass to 2 in (5 cm). Draw a circle on the cardboard. Mark six points, 2 in (5 cm) apart, around the circle.

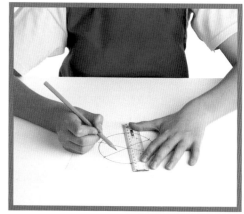

2 Draw a line between each pair of opposite points, so the three lines cross in the center of the circle. Cut out the circle.

**3** Trace a segment of the circle. Glue it onto cardboard and cut it out. Trace the shape on each color of paper and cut it out.

**4** Glue the pieces of colored paper to the circle of cardboard in this order: red, orange, yellow, green, blue, and purple.

**5** Punch a hole in the center of the circle with the tip of the scissors.* Push the pencil through the hole, as shown.

## SPINNING COLORS

*Spin the color wheel fast and watch what happens. Which color or colors can you see? When the wheel spins fast, your eyes and brain working together cannot see each color separately, so the colors blur together to make a different color.*

*As the color wheel slows down, the blurring lessens, and your eyes and brain can pick out the different colors again. Try making other wheels in just two or three colors. Do you always see the same color when you spin them?*

*Ask an adult to help you.

31